Finding S :
The Great
Alphabet Hunt

Paula Curtis Taylorson

illustrated by Caterina Cozza

Finding S : The Great Alphabet Hunt

Printed in the United States of America

A 2 Z Press LLC

PO Box 582

Deleon Springs, FL 32130

bestlittleonlinebookstore.com

sizemore3630@aol.com

440-241-3126

ISBN: 978-1-954191-20-4

Dedication

Thank you to those who read to me and those who listened to me read.

This book belongs to :

_____

She is **sensible**
and **she's serene**.

And when **she's strolling** people **stare**.

They **shout**, "It's **Señorita** Margharita, the **Spanish** dancer from Bel Air."

The **sellers** in the **shopping** mall **sneak** a peak as **she** puts **S** words in her cart.

Saving money on her weekly **selections** is **something** of an art!

She's **seeking** out a **sweetheart's** gift for her boyfriend who is also **Spanish**.

Perhaps he'd like **some skates** or **skis**, or a **spell** to make him vanish!

Oh now that's a lovely **swimsuit** for
me for **swimming** in the **salty sea**
on my **summer** long vacation!
They're on **special** offer? "I'll take three!"

Suddenly, **she sees** a **stunning** parasol for **strutting** through the **sweltering** city parks.

And then she **snaps** up a **snow**-white **Siamese** cat and a **splendid Saint** Bernard that barks.

Pointing to a **splendiferous spotty sweater,**
she shouts, "I **simply** must have that!"

"And a **Scottish skirt** that's called a kilt to match
this **scarlet scarf** and Tam o' **shanter** hat."

Still searching for that **sensational** gift
for her love, **Señor Sergio** Manuel,

she spies a **solid silver** necklace for herself
and **some** earrings made from **shell**.

This **shopping spree** is **such** thirsty work.
Perhaps I'll have a **smoothie** or a **sip** of tea.

A **small slice** of **strawberry
sponge** cake might be nice.
Oh there's just one **seat** left for me!

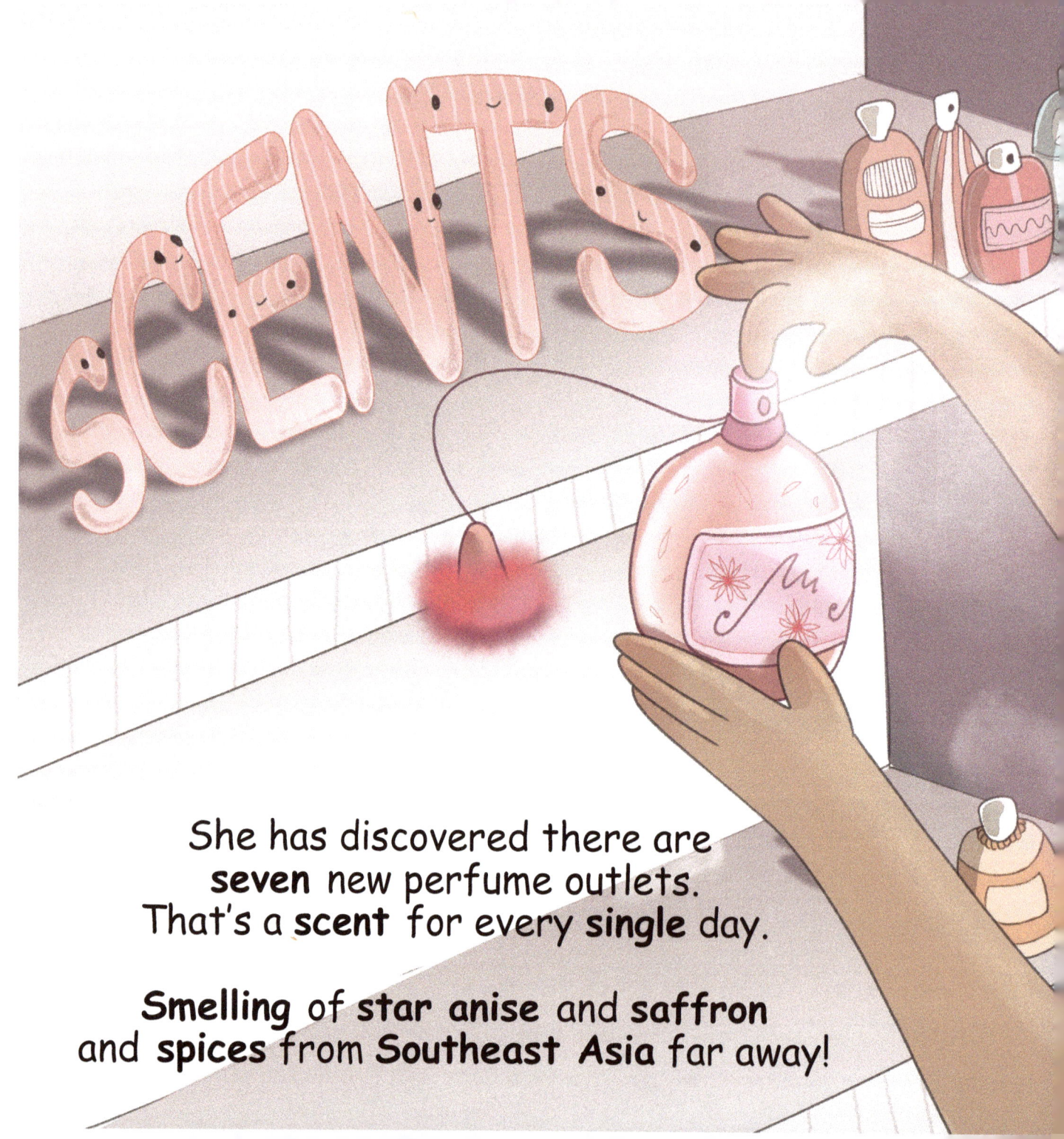

She has discovered there are
seven new perfume outlets.
That's a **scent** for every **single** day.

Smelling of **star anise** and **saffron**
and **spices** from **Southeast Asia** far away!

Sergio is **sure** to be **satisfied**
with a **sleek** and **smart** business **suit.**

But just look and **see** how **stylish** I am
in these **stiletto sandals,** they're **so** cute!

Which **store** shall I go in?
There are **seventy – seven shops** to choose.

There's a **stationers** and **saddlery**
and **several selling shiny sassy shoes.**

I **shall** have to buy that **suitcase** and the **sporty shoulder** bag that matches.

I'd better get a **smashing sewing** kit too, in case my **super skinny** jeans need patches!

I **suppose** my **Sergio** would look **sublime**
with **six** pairs of **stripey, sheep** wool **socks**

and a **sky** blue **shirt** with a matching tie, or
how about a **surprise** 'I Love You' jack-in-a-box?

SWEETIE

It's **safe** to **say** I've made a decision.
A **spectacular** wedding dress it **should** be, **sí**.

Made from **satin** with **sequins** and
simple bows and **Sergio** can **settle** for me!

The End

My Very Own 'S' Words:

_____

_____

_____

_____

_____

_____

_____

_____

_____

_____

Glossary

Page 1. **She** : referring to a female person
She's : a contracted word for she is
Sensible : using good judgment, good decisions
Serene : calm, quiet, peaceful, unruffled

Page 2. **Strolling** : walk slowly from place to place
Stare : to look at intently especially
with eyes wide open
Shout : talk loudly and energetically
Señorita : Spanish for girl or woman, female
Spanish : a nationality

Page. 4. **Sellers** : someone who exchanges goods for money
Shopping mall : an area with many stores that
sell items to buyers
Sneak : to do something without others knowing
S : a letter

Page 5. **Saving** : to reduce the amount of money spent
Selections : items being bought
Something : a certain or unspecified object
or idea or opinion

Page 7. **Seeking** : to search, look for
Sweetheart's : a beloved person, kind
Some : a certain amount or less than
all of a thing or thought
Skates : a boot with a blade or wheels
on the bottom to glide along the ground or floor
Skis : one of a pair of long, slender runners made
of wood, plastic, or metal used in gliding over snow
Spell : use magic to make something happen, have
a strong emotional effect on someone

Page 8. **Swimsuit** : clothing for swimming
Swimming : to move in the water using one's arms and legs
Salty : water with salt, the chemical sodium chloride
Sea : large bodies of salty water
Summer : season of the year that is usually warm
Special : something unique or peculiar to a thing or person

Page 10. **Suddenly** : happening quickly or unexpectedly
Stunning : of striking beauty or excellence
Strutting : to walk with a vain, pompous bearing, as with head erect and chest thrown out, as if expecting to impress observers
Sweltering : excessive heat

Page 13. **Snaps** : to grab quickly
Snow-white : white very white in color
Siamese : a cat originally from the country Siam
Splendid : magnificent, beautiful, grand, admirable, good, brilliant
Saint Bernard : a large working dog

Page 14. **Splendiferous** : another word for splendid, magnificent, fine
Spotty : irregular or uneven quality or character, spots
Sweater : clothing that is knitted with yarn
Simply : something plain and sincere

Page 15. **Scottish** : something or someone related to the country, Scotland
Skirt : the one- piece garment or part of a gown, dress, slip, or coat that extends downward from the waist and not joined between the legs, worn especially by women and girls
Scarlet : red in color

Page 15.(Continued) **Scarf** : a long, broad strip of
wool, silk, lace, or other material worn about
the neck, shoulders, or head, for ornament or
protection against cold, drafts

Tam o' **shanter** hat : a flat bonnet, originally
made of wool hand-knitted in one piece, stretched
on a wooden disc to give the distinctive flat shape

Page 16. **Still** : at this or that time, as
previously decided
Searching : to really look hard for something
Sensational : extraordinarily good,
conspicuously excellent, phenomenal
Señor Sergio Manuel : Spanish man or boy
Spies : to discover or find out by close observation
to see what one wants, to catch sight of suddenly
Solid : having the interior completely filled up,
free from cavities, not hollow

Silver : a white, ductile metallic element, used
for making mirrors, coins, ornaments, table
utensils, photographic chemicals, conductors
Shell : a hard outer covering of an animal,
as the hard
case of a mollusk, or either half of the
case of a bivalve mollusk

Page 19. **Shopping** : to go into stores to buy items
Spree : a spell or sustained period of
unrestrained activity of a particular kind
Such : of the kind, character, degree, or extent of
that or those indicated or implied

Smoothie : a drink made from fruit and a thick beverage
of fruit pureed in a blender with ice and milk, yogurt, or juice
Sip : to drink a liquid a little at a time, take small tastes of

Page 19. (Continued) **Small** : of limited size; of comparatively restricted dimensions; not big; little-slender, thin, or narrow
Slice : a part or portion of something
Strawberry : a fruit
Sponge : food, light cake made with egg whites, flour, and sugar
Seat : a chair, place to sit and rest

Page 20. **Seven** : a number
Scent : an odor noted by smelling
Single : one
Smelling : to perceive something with the nose, an odor
Star anise : is a spice made from the fruit of the Chinese evergreen tree
Saffron : an orange-colored condiment consisting of its dried stigmas, used to color and flavor foods
Spices : any of a class of pungent or aromatic substances of vegetable origin, as pepper, cinnamon, or cloves used as seasoning, preservatives
Southeast Asia : a country

Page 22. **Sure** : free of doubt, certain of something, convinced, positive
Satisfied : content, happy with something or an outcome
Sleek : smooth or glossy, as hair, trim and graceful; finely contoured
Smart : intelligent
Suit : clothes, formal clothes
See : to look at something using one's eyes
Stylish : fashionable, smart dressed
Stiletto : high heeled shoes
Sandals : a shoe consisting of a sole of leather or other material fastened to the foot by thongs or straps
So : in the way or manner indicated, described, or implied

Page 25. **Store** : a place that sells items
Seventy - seven : a number
Shops : buildings with items to sell
Stationers : a person who sells the materials
used in writing, as paper, pens, pencils, and ink
Saddlery : a person who sells the materials used
in riding horses, saddles, bridles, clothes
Several : being more than two but fewer
than many in number or kind
Selling : the act of taking money for items
Shiny : to give forth or glow with light, shed
or cast light. to be bright with reflected light
Sassy : pert, boldly smart; saucy
Shoes : an external covering for the human foot, usually of leather
and consisting of a more or less stiff or heavy sole and a lighter upper
part ending a short distance above, at, or below the ankle

Page 27. **Shall** : plan to, intend to, or expect to, will
have to, is determined to, or definitely will
Suitcase : a usually rectangular piece of luggage
especially for carrying clothes while traveling
Sporty : flashy; showy smart in dress, behavior
Shoulder : the part of each side of the body in humans
at the base of the neck to the region where
the arm attaches to the body

Page 29. **Smashing** : excellent, wonderful
Sewing : to join or attach by stitches, to make or
repair a garment by such means, to enclose or
secure with stitches
Super : of the highest degree, power,
of an extreme or excessive degree
Skinny : very lean or thin

Page 31. **Suppose** : to believe or assume as true; take for granted
Sublime : elevated or lofty in thought or Language supreme or outstanding
Six : a number
Stripey : something with a pattern of stipes or lines
Sheep : farm animal
Socks : a short stocking usually reaching to the calf or just above the ankle
Sky blue : blue a color the color of the space above the earth, the blue color of the sky
Shirt : a long- or short-sleeved garment for the upper part of the body, usually lightweight and having a collar and a front opening
Surprise : something unexpected, startled

Page 33. **Safe** : secure from liability to harm, injury, danger, or risk
Say : to utter or express words or thoughts
Spectacular : marked by or given to an impressive, large-scale display, dramatically daring or thrilling
Should be : must; ought, used to indicate duty
Sí :Spanish for 'yes'
Satin : a fabric often having a glossy surface and a soft, slippery texture
Sequins : a small shining disk or spangle used for ornamentation, as on clothing, accessories, or theatrical costume
Simple : not fancy or complicated
Settle : to appoint, fix, or resolve definitely and conclusively; agree upon as time, price, or conditions, to place in a desired state or in order

Paula Curtis-Taylorson Lives in Marston Mortaine England. She is a full-time secondary school teacher of English and English Literature. She was amongst the first of the initial students to graduate from the Uk's first BA (Hons) Creative Writing Program at the University of Bedfordshire.

Her first love is poetry and rhyme and she works hard to inspire and teach appreciation of the subject to all age groups. Many of her students have gone on to be successful writers.